2022
FAMILY
ASTRONOMICAL
ALMANAC

For Norma Jean,
a light to all in her orbit.

Published by Bushel & Peck Books, a family-run publishing house in Fresno, California, that
believes in uplifting children with the highest standards of art, music, literature, and ideas.
Find beautiful books for gifted young minds at www.bushelandpeckbooks.com.

Type set in Josefin Sans, Avenir Next, and Pacifico.

Designed by David Miles.

All photographs and design elements licensed from Shutterstock.com.

Bushel & Peck Books is dedicated to fighting illiteracy all over the world. For every
book we sell, we donate one to a child in need—book for book. To nominate a school or
organization to receive free books, please visit www.bushelandpeckbooks.com.

LCCN: 2021946096
ISBN: 9781638190202

First Edition

Printed in the United States

10 9 8 7 6 5 4 3 2 1

NORTHERN HEMISPHERE

2022

FAMILY ASTRONOMICAL ALMANAC

A BEGINNER'S GUIDE TO SPOTTING THIS YEAR'S
ECLIPSES, METEOR SHOWERS, PLANETARY
CONJUNCTIONS & MORE!

CONTENTS

KEY

🪐 METEOR SHOWER

◎ ORBITAL MILESTONE

🪐 PLANETARY EVENT

🌙 LUNAR ECLIPSE

☀ YEAR'S BEST

INTRODUCTION

*W*elcome to the night sky! There's nothing quite so humbling and inspiring as spending an evening watching the dance of the heavens. It's even better when you do it with the people you love, which is why publishing this family guide to the events of the night sky is so exciting for us.

HOW WE CHOSE THE EVENTS

When it comes to astronomy, there is a lot to learn and a *lot* to observe! But in this book, we've picked out the most popular events that are easiest for beginner families and kids to tackle. You'll find lunar eclipses, meteor showers, and planetary conjunctions, plus we've also noted some of the most significant orbital events of the year, like solstices and equinoxes.

DO I NEED A TELESCOPE?

If you have one, great! But if not, don't worry. We purposefully selected events that don't require any special equipment to see. In place of a telescope, you might consider binoculars, but even those are optional.

A NOTE ABOUT PHOTOGRAPHS

Wherever possible, we've included photographs of the actual astronomical events. In many cases, however, photos of comparable events or artistic renderings have had to be used instead. For planetary conjunctions, some photos feature conjunctions as they appear in the sky, while others show additional details of the planets up close.

With all that said, it's time to unfold some blankets, make a cup (or gallon) of cocoa, and get ready to wonder at the majesty of the heavens above. The night sky awaits!

Happy stargazing,

Bushel & Peck Books

HOW TO USE THIS BOOK

*E*ach page of this book is designed to make it easy to find information about each astronomical event. Here's a quick tour:

DESCRIPTION: This will provide background information about the event, scientific explanations, and tips for getting the best views.

TYPE OF EVENT: In general, events are categorized as planetary events, orbital milestones, eclipses, and meteor showers.

BEST VIEWING TIME: This recommends the best time of day to catch the event. If best viewing is advised for dusk, this means dusk of the date written. If best viewing is advised for dawn, this means the early morning of the date written. If viewing can occur all night, this means the evening of the date written, running into the early morning of the next day.

DIRECTION IN SKY: This advises the general area of the sky to look in. Please note that since the Earth is turning during the night, the exact location of stars and planets in the sky changes, too. Where you find the event in the sky might be different than what's written.

MAY 26

PLANETARY EVENT

CAN BE SEEN WITH NAKED EYE

15%

CONJUNCTION OF MOON AND VENUS

Venus and the Moon will pass near each other in the night sky. Look high in the heavens in a southern direction in the early hours just before dawn. The Moon will be easy to spot, of course; the bright spot nearby is Venus.

BEST VIEWING TIME: the two hours before dawn

DIRECTION IN SKY: south

48

EVENT NAME

RADIANT:

Aries

JUN 10

ARIETIDS METEOR SHOWER 79%

The Arietids meteor shower has one of the higher meteor frequency rates, averaging over fifty meteors per hour at its peak. The shower is active from April 14 until June 24, but the day with the most intense meteor activity will be June 10. Your best chance of seeing a shooting star will be during the early morning hours just before dawn. Scientists don't yet know the source of the Arietids, and unfortunately, this year's shower will coincide with a near-full Moon, possibly making them harder to see.

BEST VIEWING TIME: **the two hours before dawn**

PEAK: **50-60 meteors per hour**

DIRECTION IN SKY: **north (though meteors can radiate across most of the sky)**

METEOR SHOWER

RECURS ANNUALLY

CAN BE SEEN WITH NAKED EYE

RADIANT: For meteor showers, we've included the radiant constellation. This is the point in the sky that the meteors will come from, and it's often what gives a meteor shower its name. But don't worry if these constellations are hard to spot in the sky—it's not necessary for enjoying the meteor shower, since meteors will radiate across most of the sky!

MOON PHASE: This icon indicates what phase the Moon will be in and its percentage of illumination. The higher the percentage, the higher the illumination and the brighter the Moon (a full moon is 100 percent illuminated, for example). Some events, like meteor showers, are harder to spot if there's a very bright moon, so keep this in mind.

PEAK: This will tell you the highest level of activity a meteor shower is expected to reach (written in meteors per hour). However, remember that this is the projected number under ideal conditions like perfect darkness and clear skies. Chances are, the number of meteors you actually see will be much fewer (though still majestic!).

TIPS FOR STARGAZING

*W*ith a little preparation, you can make a night under the stars both fun and comfortable, not to mention memorable! Here are a few tips to do just that.

MAKE A PLAN. Pick where you're going to go (see below), know how long it will take to get there, and know when the event you want to observe is forecasted to occur. There's nothing more disappointing than doing all the work to catch a celestial event, only to be too late.

GO WHERE THERE IS AS LITTLE LIGHT AS POSSIBLE. Light pollution from cities and towns can make it much harder to see what's in the night sky. Find a place that is away from artificial light, like national and state parks, farms (with permission, of course), rural roads, and other places out in the country. It might mean a bit of a drive, but it will be worth it!

DRESS WARMLY. Even summer nights can get a little chilly sometimes. Dress in layers. On especially cold winter nights, you'll want hats, gloves, and even packaged hand warmers (they're wonderful!).

EXPECT SOME WAIT TIME. Waiting for a meteor shower to start or for an eclipse to begin requires some patience. This might be especially tough for younger kids, so plan ahead and bring snacks, games, and other fun activities to pass the time.

GET COMFORTABLE. Chairs, sleeping bags, pillows, and blankets can make the night hours nice and cozy. A little hot cocoa and some cookies don't hurt, either!

GLOSSARY

*T*hroughout this book, although we've tried to keep astronomical jargon to a minimum, you might find terms you're not familiar with. Here is a list of definitions to help.

asteroid: a body made from rock and metal that orbits the Sun

blue moon: the second full moon during the same calendar month (there are none forecasted for 2022, unfortunately)

comet: a body made of rock and ice that orbits the Sun, usually with a tail of gas and debris

conjunction: when two bodies like the Moon or a planet appear especially near each other in the sky

constellation: a recognizable pattern or shape made from stars that goes by a universal name (e.g. the constellation Orion)

dawn: the twilight hours just before sunrise

dusk: the twilight hours just after sunset

full moon: the phase of the Moon when it is fully bright (*see* also "new moon" for comparison)

equinox: when the Sun is directly over the equator, resulting in equal day and night; this occurs two times per year (*see* Spring equinox on March 20 and September equinox on September 22)

gibbous: a word used to describe the Moon when it's more than half full; comes from *gibbus*, the Latin word for "humpback"

gravitational pull: the attractive force that one body exerts on another

horizon: where the sky and ground meet

lunar eclipse: when the shadow of the Earth falls on the Moon and reduces its light (see also "solar eclipse" for comparison)

meteor: a small piece of debris that burns when entering the Earth's atmosphere; also called a "shooting star"

meteor shower: a dense display of meteors, usually caused by the Earth moving through the debris trail of a comet or asteroid

meteorite: a meteor that doesn't completely burn up during its trip through the atmosphere and lands on the surface of the Earth

naked eye: with eyes only, without the aid of binoculars or telescopes

new moon: the phase of the Moon when it is completely dark (see also "full moon" for comparison)

orbit: the path a celestial body, like a planet or comet, takes around the Sun

peak: when the activity of a meteor shower is at its highest point (usually measured in meteors per hour)

radiant: the point in the sky from which a meteor shower issues (usually a constellation)

solar eclipse: when the Moon blocks the Sun and the Moon's shadow can be seen on Earth (see also "lunar eclipse" for comparison)

solstice: when the poles of the Earth are the closest or furthest away from the Sun (see "June solstice" on June 21 and "December solstice" on December 21)

waxing: when the amount of the Moon that is bright is increasing

waning: when the amount of the Moon that is bright is decreasing

Book Sources / Suggested Reading

- solarsystem.nasa.gov
- theskylive.com
- in-the-sky.org
- eclipse.gsfc.nasa.gov
- earthsky.org
- www.universeguide.com
- en.wikipedia.org
- www.space.com
- starwalk.space
- www.spacereference.org
- skyandtelescope.org
- sservi.nasa.gov
- www.mooninfo.org

CALENDAR

*T*he following pages contain daily entries for each of the astronomical events scheduled to occur in 2022. Catch a meteor shower or spot a planet for the first time. The night sky is yours!

JAN 3

QUADRANTIDS METEOR SHOWER

1%

METEOR SHOWER

RECURS ANNUALLY

CAN BE SEEN WITH NAKED EYE

One of the best meteor showers of the year, the Quadrantids meteor shower happens every January when the Earth passes through the orbit of an asteroid called 2003 EH1 (it's possible it might be a sort of dead comet, but scientists are still debating). The asteroid's trail is filled with debris—rocks, dust, bits of other asteroids—that burn up as they enter the Earth's atmosphere. The meteor shower usually lasts for a few hours, and then Earth must wait for another year to see it again.

BEST VIEWING TIME: during the night and predawn

PEAK: 60-200 meteors per hour!

DIRECTION IN SKY: north (though meteors can radiate across most of the sky)

PERIHELION

The perihelion is the point in a planet's orbit when the planet is its closest to the Sun. Earth's perihelion occurs every year in January. You might wonder how Earth can be closer to the Sun at one time of the year and further away from it at another time. Doesn't it move in a circle? Not exactly. Earth's orbit is actually an ellipse, which means it moves in a slightly oval shape as it circles the Sun. As a result, it's a tiny bit closer to the Sun at some times, and a tiny bit farther away at other times.

ORBITAL
MILESTONE

RECURS
ANNUALLY

Aphelion
July

Perihelion
January

152 million km   147 million km

JAN
5

DID YOU KNOW?

Jupiter is twice as big as *all* the other planets put together!

10%

CONJUNCTION OF MOON AND JUPITER

PLANETARY
EVENT

CAN BE
SEEN WITH
NAKED EYE

Jupiter and the Moon will be extremely close together in the night sky, making it easy to spot both at once. You can see them with the naked eye or with binoculars, but they might be too far apart to see through a telescope. Look for a bright point right near the Moon—that's Jupiter!

BEST VIEWING TIME: **between dusk and nightfall**

DIRECTION IN SKY: **southwest**

RADIANT:

Ursa Minor

98%

γ-URSAE MINORIDS METEOR SHOWER

Though it occurs from January 15 to January 22, the peak viewing time for the γ-Ursae Minorids will be during the early morning of January 19. Look for the constellation Ursa Minor (the little bear, whose tail is Polaris, the North Star) and expect to see meteors radiating outwards from that area. This particular shower is not as intense as others, but there's still a good chance of seeing a shooting star.

BEST VIEWING TIME: during the night and predawn

PEAK: 3 meteors per hour

DIRECTION IN SKY: north (though meteors can radiate across most of the sky)

METEOR SHOWER

RECURS ANNUALLY

CAN BE SEEN WITH NAKED EYE

JAN 29

DID YOU KNOW? Mars is much smaller than Earth. If Earth were the size of a dime, Mars would only look like an aspirin tablet sitting next to it. But while Earth has only one moon, Mars has two!

PLANETARY EVENT

CAN BE SEEN WITH NAKED EYE

10%

CONJUNCTION OF MOON AND MARS

Mars and the Moon will be close together in the night sky. You can see them with the naked eye or with binoculars, but they might be too far apart to see through a telescope. Look for a bright point right near the Moon—that's Mars!

BEST VIEWING TIME: the two hours before dawn

DIRECTION IN SKY: southeast

VENUS AT ITS BRIGHTEST

Named after the Roman God of love, Venus is the second planet from the sun and one of Earth's neighbors. This will be one of the best times of the year to see the planet Venus since it will be at its brightest. But rather than view it at dusk, the best time to spot it is actually just before sunrise. Look towards the southeast, a little above the horizon.

PLANETARY EVENT

CAN BE SEEN WITH NAKED EYE

. . . .

BEST VIEWING TIME: just before dawn

. . . .

DIRECTION IN SKY: southeast

. . . .

FEB 12

CONJUNCTION OF VENUS AND MARS

84%

Venus and Mars will pass very near each other in the night sky, making them a little easier to pick out. During the early morning—about two hours before sunrise—look due south in the sky for two bright points next to each other.

PLANETARY EVENT

CAN BE SEEN WITH NAKED EYE

BEST VIEWING TIME: **the two hours before dawn**

DIRECTION IN SKY: **southeast**

Venus, Earth, and Mars are all neighbors, and yet the temperature on Venus's surface is hot enough to melt lead, while the surface on Mars is so cold that water instantly freezes. Earth is a pretty good place to call home!

FEB 27

13%

CONJUNCTION OF MOON, VENUS, AND MARS

Mars, Venus, and the Moon will all appear near each other in the early morning sky, a couple of hours before dawn. Look for the Moon, then locate two bright points nearby.

BEST VIEWING TIME: the two hours before dawn

DIRECTION IN SKY: south

PLANETARY EVENT

CAN BE SEEN WITH NAKED EYE

MAR 12

69%

CONJUNCTION OF VENUS AND MARS

PLANETARY
EVENT

CAN BE
SEEN WITH
NAKED EYE

Though over 70 million miles away from each other, Venus and Mars will appear near each other in the early-morning sky. Look southeast during the hours just before dawn. Venus is typically the brighter of the two planets, while Mars will have a reddish hue.

BEST VIEWING TIME: just before dawn

DIRECTION IN SKY: southeast

MARCH EQUINOX

Also called the *spring equinox* or the *Vernal equinox*, the March equinox marks the point that the Sun aligns perfectly with the Earth's equator. Since the Earth is usually tilted towards or away from the Sun—the cause of the seasons—this perfect alignment during the equinox is unique. On this day, the Sun will rise from the exact east and set in the exact west. It will also produce almost exactly twelve hours of day and twelve hours of night in most parts of the world, which is where the term comes from: *aequus* (Latin for "equal") and *nox* (Latin for "night"). The March equinox marks the official beginning of spring.

ORBITAL
MILESTONE

RECURS
ANNUALLY

EQUINOX
21 March

Earth's orbit

SOLSTICE
22 December

SOLSTICE
21 June

EQUINOX
23 September

MAR 27

CONJUNCTION OF MOON AND MARS

PLANETARY EVENT

CAN BE SEEN WITH NAKED EYE

Mars and the Moon will be extremely close together in the night sky, making it easy to spot both at once. You can see them with the naked eye or with binoculars, but they might be too far apart to see through a telescope. Look for a bright point right near the Moon—that's Mars!

....

BEST VIEWING TIME: the two hours before dawn

....

DIRECTION IN SKY: southeast

....

CONJUNCTION OF MOON, VENUS, AND SATURN

16%

PLANETARY EVENT

The Moon, Venus, and Saturn will *all* be near each other in the night sky! Binoculars might make it easier to see. Point them towards the Moon, which should be in a southeastern direction just above the horizon, and look for two bright points nearby.

CAN BE SEEN WITH NAKED EYE

BEST VIEWING TIME: the two hours before dawn

DIRECTION IN SKY: southeast

MAR 29

PLANETARY
EVENT

CAN BE
SEEN WITH
NAKED EYE

9%

CONJUNCTION OF VENUS AND SATURN

Venus and Saturn will appear near each other in the early morning. Look south-southeast for two bright points partway up above the horizon. Saturn has a much larger orbit than Venus (it's millions more miles away from the Sun), but the two do align in the night sky on a regular basis. Binoculars aren't required but will sure help!

BEST VIEWING TIME: **the two hours before dawn**

DIRECTION IN SKY: **south-southeast**

DID YOU KNOW?
Saturn has sixty-two moons. Sixty-two! Scientists speculate that some might even have conditions that could support life.

CONJUNCTION OF MARS AND SATURN

10%

Mars and Saturn will be near one other in the morning sky, just above the horizon. Look directly south in the two hours just before dawn for two bright points. Mars will be somewhat reddish in color, which should help you tell the pair apart.

BEST VIEWING TIME: the two hours before dawn

DIRECTION IN SKY: southeast

PLANETARY
EVENT

CAN BE
SEEN WITH
NAKED EYE

LYRIDS METEOR SHOWER

61%

Less active than the Quadrantids but more so than the γ-Ursae Minorids, the Lyrid meteor shower produces a peak of seventeen meteors per hour. This will be easiest to observe during the early morning hours before dawn on April 22, though the shower will still be happening (with less intensity) between April 16 and April 25. The comet C/1861 G1 is responsible for the Lyrid meteor shower, its trail of rocky particles burning up in the Earth's atmosphere as the Earth passes through.

METEOR SHOWER

RECURS ANNUALLY

CAN BE SEEN WITH NAKED EYE

BEST VIEWING TIME: early hours just before dawn

PEAK: 17 meteors per hour

DIRECTION IN SKY: north-northeast (though meteors can radiate across most of the sky)

RADIANT:

Puppis

APR
23

π-PUPPIDS METEOR SHOWER

50%

Since it will occur close to a new Moon this year, the π-Puppid meteor shower will be particularly visible in the sky. For best viewing, look in a southwestern direction after dusk on the evening of April 23 (though the shower will happen between April 15 and April 28). The comet whose trail is responsible for the shower is 26P/Grigg-Skjellerup, which was first discovered in 1902. The comet was later visited in 1992 by the Giotto probe, an unmanned spacecraft from the European Space Agency.

METEOR SHOWER

RECURS ANNUALLY

CAN BE SEEN WITH NAKED EYE

BEST VIEWING TIME: just after dusk

PEAK: 10 meteors per hour

DIRECTION IN SKY: southwest (though meteors can radiate across most of the sky)

APR 24

PLANETARY
EVENT

CAN BE
SEEN WITH
NAKED EYE

39%

CONJUNCTION OF MOON AND SATURN

Saturn and the Moon will be extremely close together in the night sky, making it easy to spot both at once. Binoculars might make it easier to see. Point them towards the Moon, which should be in a southern direction just above the horizon, and look for a bright point nearby.

BEST VIEWING TIME: the two hours before dawn

DIRECTION IN SKY: south

APR
25

 28%

CONJUNCTION OF MOON AND MARS

You can see both Mars and the Moon when they're extremely close together in the night sky on April 25. Look for a bright point right near the Moon—that's Mars!

PLANETARY EVENT

CAN BE SEEN WITH NAKED EYE

....

BEST VIEWING TIME: the two hours before dawn

....

DIRECTION IN SKY: south-southeast

....

APR 27

PLANETARY
EVENT

CAN BE
SEEN WITH
NAKED EYE

12%

CONJUNCTION OF MOON AND JUPITER

This will be a good chance to try to see Jupiter, since it will be near the Moon, but the Moon will be relatively dark (only a small crescent at the time). Look for a bright point near the Moon above the eastern horizon just before dawn.

BEST VIEWING TIME: **the two hours before dawn**

DIRECTION IN SKY: **east**

**MAY
6**

27%

☀ η-AQUARIIDS METEOR SHOWER

The η-Aquariid meteor shower happens every year when the Earth passes through the trail of none other than Halley's Comet, arguably the most famous comet in space. The peak of the meteor shower will occur around May 6 and will be most visible between the hours of 3:00 am and 5:30 am in a southeastern direction. Halley's Comet visits the Earth roughly every seventy-five years, and stargazers first noticed it as early as 240 BC (though it wasn't until 1705 that Edmond Halley realized it was a recurring visitor).

BEST VIEWING TIME: between 3:00 am and 5:30 am

PEAK: 40 meteors per hour

DIRECTION IN SKY: southeast (though meteors can radiate across most of the sky)

METEOR
SHOWER

RECURS
ANNUALLY

CAN BE
SEEN WITH
NAKED EYE

MAY 8

45%

METEOR
SHOWER

RECURS
ANNUALLY

CAN BE
SEEN WITH
NAKED EYE

η-LYRIDS METEOR SHOWER

One of the quieter meteor showers, the η-Lyrid meteor shower happens when the Earth passes through the trail of comet C/1983 H1. The shower will be visible all night, with peak visibility happening around 5:00 am.

BEST VIEWING TIME: **early hours just before dawn**

PEAK: **3 meteors per hour**

DIRECTION IN SKY: **northeast (though meteors can radiate across most of the sky)**

☀ TOTAL LUNAR ECLIPSE

99%

Lunar eclipses happen with regularity, though a *total* lunar eclipse is more rare. This happens when the Earth moves between the Moon and the Sun, casting a shadow and causing the Moon to darken or turn red in color. This particular eclipse will be visible throughout America, Europe, and Africa. It will begin around 7:30 pm PST/10:30 pm EST Sunday night. Gradually, as the Moon moves into Earth's shadow, the eclipse will grow until the Moon is in total darkness by 8:30 pm PST/11:30 pm EST. Unlike solar eclipses, a lunar eclipse can be viewed safely with the naked eye.

LUNAR ECLIPSE

CAN BE SEEN WITH NAKED EYE

BEST VIEWING TIME: Between 7:30 pm PST/10:30 pm EST and 9:30 pm PST/12:30 am EST

53%

CONJUNCTION OF MOON AND SATURN

PLANETARY EVENT

CAN BE SEEN WITH NAKED EYE

Saturn and the Moon will be neighbords in the sky. Binoculars might make it easier to see. Point them towards the Moon, which should be in a southern direction just above the horizon, and look for a bright point nearby.

BEST VIEWING TIME: the two hours before dawn

DIRECTION IN SKY: south

CONJUNCTION OF MOON, MARS, AND JUPITER

32%

Mars, Jupiter, *and* the Moon will all appear near each other in the early morning sky a couple of hours before dawn. Look for the Moon, then locate two bright points nearby. Fortunately, the Moon will be a waning crescent, so its light should have minimal interference.

PLANETARY EVENT

CAN BE SEEN WITH NAKED EYE

BEST VIEWING TIME: the two hours before dawn

DIRECTION IN SKY: south

CONJUNCTION OF MOON AND VENUS

PLANETARY EVENT

CAN BE SEEN WITH NAKED EYE

Venus and the Moon will pass near each other in the night sky. Look high in the heavens in a southern direction in the early hours just before dawn. The Moon will be easy to spot, of course; the bright spot nearby is Venus.

....

BEST VIEWING TIME: the two hours before dawn

....

DIRECTION IN SKY: south

....

☀ ARIETIDS METEOR SHOWER

79%

The Arietids meteor shower has one of the higher meteor frequency rates, averaging over fifty meteors per hour at its peak. The shower is active from April 14 until June 24, but the day with the most intense meteor activity will be June 10. Your best chance of seeing a shooting star will be during the early morning hours just before dawn. Scientists don't yet know the source of the Arietids, and unfortunately, this year's shower will coincide with a near-full Moon, possibly making them harder to see.

BEST VIEWING TIME: the two hours before dawn

PEAK: 50-60 meteors per hour

DIRECTION IN SKY: north (though meteors can radiate across most of the sky)

METEOR SHOWER

RECURS ANNUALLY

CAN BE SEEN WITH NAKED EYE

JUN 18

78%

CONJUNCTION OF MOON AND SATURN

Saturn and the Moon will be extremely close together in the night sky, making it easy to spot both at once. Binoculars might make Saturn easier to see. Look in a southern direction just above the horizon.

BEST VIEWING TIME: the two hours before dawn

DIRECTION IN SKY: south

PLANETARY
EVENT

CAN BE
SEEN WITH
NAKED EYE

JUNE SOLSTICE

This marks the first day of summer in the Northern Hemisphere (hence it is sometimes called the summer solstice). It occurs when the northern pole of the Earth is pointed most directly at the Sun. As a result, it is also the longest day of the year, with cities in the extreme north experiencing daylight nearly all day long—twenty-two hours of light in Fairbanks, Alaska, and a full twenty-four hours in Mumansk, Russia—and cities further south still having longer-than-usual light—sixteen hours in Paris, and fifteen hours in New York. So get up early and play long into the night; you'll have plenty of light!

ORBITAL
MILESTONE

RECURS
ANNUALLY

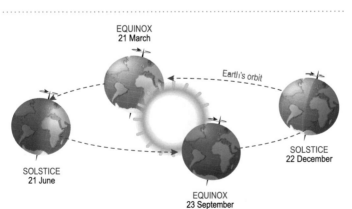

EQUINOX
21 March

Earth's orbit

SOLSTICE
22 December

SOLSTICE
21 June

EQUINOX
23 September

JUN 21

CONJUNCTION OF MOON AND JUPITER

46%

PLANETARY EVENT

CAN BE SEEN WITH NAKED EYE

Look for a bright point near the Moon above the eastern horizon just before dawn.

BEST VIEWING TIME: the two hours before dawn (which is early on the summer solstice!)

DIRECTION IN SKY: southeast

DID YOU KNOW? **A year on Mars would last 687 Earth days.**

36%

CONJUNCTION OF MOON AND MARS

Mars and the Moon will be extremely close together in the night sky. You can see them with the naked eye or with binoculars, but they might be too far apart to see through a telescope. Look for a reddish, bright point right near the Moon.

....

BEST VIEWING TIME: the two hours before dawn

....

DIRECTION IN SKY: southwest

....

PLANETARY
EVENT

CAN BE
SEEN WITH
NAKED EYE

2%

BOOTIDS METEOR SHOWER

As the Earth passes through the trail of comet 7P/Pons-Winnecke, expect to see the Bootid meteor shower between June 22 and July 2. The peak will occur on June 27, with the best time to view soon after nightfall (though the shower will be visible above the horizon all night). Comet Pons-Winnecke was discovered in 1819. Scientists estimate that its head is over three miles wide! Though there are usually only one or two meteors per hour even at the shower's peak, the Bootid shower is known for producing slower moving meteors than other showers.

BEST VIEWING TIME: right after dusk

PEAK: 1-2 meteors per hour

DIRECTION IN SKY: northeast (though meteors can radiate across most of the sky)

METEOR
SHOWER

RECURS
ANNUALLY

CAN BE
SEEN WITH
NAKED EYE

APHELION

25%

The aphelion is the point in a planet's orbit when the planet is furthest from the Sun. Earth's aphelion occurs every year in July, whereas its perihelion—the point it's *closest* to the Sun—occurs in January (see the Perihelion on January 3). During the aphelion, the Sun will technically appear smaller in the sky than on any other day. However, since it's only about 3 percent smaller than usual, it's unlikely you'll notice!

ORBITAL
MILESTONE

RECURS
ANNUALLY

Aphelion
July

Perihelion
January

152 million km   147 million km

JUL 15

Saturn's density is actually less than that of water. If there were a bathtub the size of the solar system filled with water, Saturn would float!

95%

CONJUNCTION OF MOON AND SATURN

Saturn and the Moon will be extremely close together in the night sky. Look towards the Moon, which should be in a southern direction just above the horizon, and search for a bright point nearby.

BEST VIEWING TIME: **the two hours before dawn**

DIRECTION IN SKY: **south**

PLANETARY
EVENT

CAN BE
SEEN WITH
NAKED EYE

CONJUNCTION OF MOON AND JUPITER

This is another chance to catch Jupiter passing nearby the Moon. Unlike on June 21, the Moon during this conjunction will be nearly full, however, so its bright light might make it slightly more difficult. Look for a bright point near the Moon above the southern horizon just before dawn.

PLANETARY EVENT

CAN BE SEEN WITH NAKED EYE

BEST VIEWING TIME: the two hours before dawn

DIRECTION IN SKY: south

JUL 21

DID YOU KNOW? Billions of years ago, Mars was likely a warm planet that even had oceans and rain!

41%

CONJUNCTION OF MOON AND MARS

PLANETARY EVENT

CAN BE SEEN WITH NAKED EYE

You can see them with the naked eye or with binoculars, but they might be too far apart to see through a telescope. Look for a bright point right near the Moon—that's Mars!

BEST VIEWING TIME: the two hours before dawn

DIRECTION IN SKY: south-southeast

JUL
29

PISCIS AUSTRINIDS
METEOR SHOWER

1%

Occurring between July 15 through August 10 but with a peak on July 29, the Piscis Austrinids happen when the Earth passes through a space trail of debris left from an unknown object (some scientists think it may be a comet or asteroid that has since disintegrated). This particular shower is usually somewhat faint, so viewing is best during the darkest hours of the night. Fortunately, there will be almost no Moon this year, so light interference should be minimal.

BEST VIEWING TIME: **after midnight**

PEAK: **5 meteors per hour**

DIRECTION IN SKY: **south (though meteors can radiate across most of the sky)**

METEOR
SHOWER

RECURS
ANNUALLY

CAN BE
SEEN WITH
NAKED EYE

RADIANT: Aquarius

3%

SOUTHERN δ-AQUARIIDS METEOR SHOWER

The Southern δ-Aquariids (not to be confused with the η-Aquariids on May 6) occur around the same time as the Piscis Austrinids and are usually a little easier to see. Producing around twenty-five meteors per hour at its peak, the Aquariids happen between July 12 and August 23 with a peak on July 30. The shower begins when the Earth enters the orbit of comet P/2008 Y12 (SOHO). SOHO takes over five years to complete an orbit around the Sun, and though its orbit takes it very close to the Earth, scientists say that simulations don't forecast a future collision. Whew!

METEOR SHOWER

RECURS ANNUALLY

CAN BE SEEN WITH NAKED EYE

BEST VIEWING TIME: **2–3 hours before sunrise**

PEAK: **25 meteors per hour**

DIRECTION IN SKY: **east (though meteors can radiate across most of the sky)**

JUL 30

α-CAPRICORNIDS METEOR SHOWER

Active from July 3 until August 15 but with a peak on July 30, the Capricornids radiate from a point near—you guessed it—the Capricornus constellation. At its peak, the shower produces around only five meteors per hour, but since Capricornus will be above the horizon most of the night, the shower can be viewed during all nighttime hours. The best viewing will be in a southern direction shortly after midnight. The comet trail responsible for the meteor shower belongs to comet 169P/NEAT, which scientists believe might have broken off from the same celestial body as P/2008 T12 (SOHO) nearly 3,000 years ago.

METEOR SHOWER

RECURS ANNUALLY

CAN BE SEEN WITH NAKED EYE

....

BEST VIEWING TIME: after midnight, though visible all night

....

PEAK: 5 meteors per hour

....

DIRECTION IN SKY: south (though meteors can radiate across most of the sky)

....

**PLANETARY
EVENT**

**CAN BE
SEEN WITH
NAKED EYE**

100%

CONJUNCTION OF MOON AND SATURN

Saturn and the Moon will once again be extremely close together in the night sky. Binoculars might make Saturn easier to see. Point them towards the Moon, which should be in a southeastern direction just above the horizon, and look for a bright point nearby.

BEST VIEWING TIME: the two hours before dawn

DIRECTION IN SKY: southeast

AUG 13

☀ PERSEIDS METEOR SHOWER

 97%

Like the Quadrantids, the Perseids shower is one of the best meteor showers of the year, producing around 150 meteors per hour during its peak. The shower occurs between July 17 and August 24, with the highest rate of meteors happening on August 13. Unfortunately, the Moon will be nearly full during this year's Perseids and might make viewing a little more challenging. The Perseids occur when the Earth passes through the orbit of comet 109P/Swift-Tuttle, which was first discovered in 1862. It's a massive comet with a head nearly sixteen miles across!

METEOR SHOWER

BEST VIEWING TIME: just before dawn, though visible all night

RECURS ANNUALLY

PEAK: 150 meteors per hour!

CAN BE SEEN WITH NAKED EYE

DIRECTION IN SKY: northeast (though meteors can radiate across most of the sky)

AUG 15

85%

CONJUNCTION OF MOON AND JUPITER

Look for a bright point near the Moon above the southeastern horizon just before dawn.

PLANETARY EVENT

CAN BE SEEN WITH NAKED EYE

BEST VIEWING TIME: **the two hours before dawn**

DIRECTION IN SKY: **southeast**

RADIANT:

Cygnus

AUG
18

κ-CYGNIDS METEOR SHOWER

57%

Though among the less dramatic meteor showers, the Cygnids are a last chance to catch some shooting stars during the warm summer. The shower occurs between August 3 and August 25. Its peak, on August 18, can produce around five meteors per hour. Because of its close timing to the Perseids, early observers didn't realize it was a separate meteor shower until 1877.

BEST VIEWING TIME: **before midnight, though visible all night**

PEAK: **5 meteors per hour**

DIRECTION IN SKY: **north-northwest (though meteors can radiate across most of the sky)**

METEOR SHOWER

RECURS ANNUALLY

CAN BE SEEN WITH NAKED EYE

AUG 19

47%

CONJUNCTION OF MOON AND MARS

PLANETARY EVENT

CAN BE SEEN WITH NAKED EYE

Look for a bright point right near the Moon—that's Mars!

BEST VIEWING TIME: the two hours before dawn

DIRECTION IN SKY: southeast

SEP 1

AURIGIDS METEOR SHOWER

 26%

At their height, the Aurigids produce around six meteors per hour, with a peak occurring on September 1 (though the shower happens between August 28 and September 5). The meteor shower begins when the Earth moves through the orbit of comet C/1911 N1 (Kiess), which was first discovered in 1911. Fortunately, the Moon this year will be only a quarter-moon, so visibility should be a little better than usual.

METEOR SHOWER

RECURS ANNUALLY

CAN BE SEEN WITH NAKED EYE

BEST VIEWING TIME: just before dawn

PEAK: 6 meteors per hour

DIRECTION IN SKY: east-northeast (though meteors can radiate across most of the sky)

SEP 8

95%

CONJUNCTION OF MOON AND SATURN

PLANETARY EVENT

CAN BE SEEN WITH NAKED EYE

Look towards the Moon, which should be in a southeastern direction above the horizon, and search for a bright point nearby.

....

BEST VIEWING TIME: **after dusk but before midnight**

....

DIRECTION IN SKY: **southeast**

....

CONJUNCTION OF MOON AND JUPITER

98%

Search for a bright point near the Moon above the southern horizon around midnight.

BEST VIEWING TIME: **midnight**

DIRECTION IN SKY: **south**

PLANETARY EVENT

CAN BE SEEN WITH NAKED EYE

SEP
16

DID YOU KNOW? It takes Mars almost twice as long as the Earth to complete an orbit around the Sun.

PLANETARY EVENT

CAN BE SEEN WITH NAKED EYE

63%

CONJUNCTION OF MOON AND MARS

Once again, Mars and the Moon will be extremely close together in the night sky, making it easy to spot both at once. You can see them with the naked eye or with binoculars, but they might be too far apart to see through a telescope. Look for a bright point right near the Moon—that's Mars! You might notice its reddish color.

BEST VIEWING TIME: the two hours before dawn

DIRECTION IN SKY: south

SEPTEMBER EQUINOX

Like its counterpart, the March equinox (see March 20), the September equinox marks the point that the Sun again aligns perfectly with the Earth's equator. As you'll recall, since the Earth is usually tilted towards or away from the Sun—the cause of the seasons—this perfect alignment during the equinox is unique. On this day, the Sun will rise from the exact east and set in the exact west. It will also produce almost exactly twelve hours of day and twelve hours of night in most parts of the world. The September equinox signals the beginning of the fall season.

ORBITAL
MILESTONE

RECURS
ANNUALLY

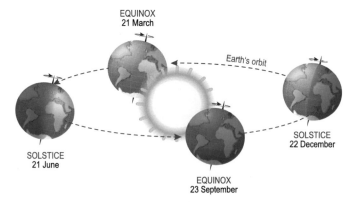

EQUINOX
21 March

Earth's orbit

SOLSTICE
22 December

SOLSTICE
21 June

EQUINOX
23 September

SEP 27

RADIANT:

Sextans

3%

SEXTANTIDS METEOR SHOWER

Occurring between September 9 and October 9, the Sextantids peak on September 27 with a climax of between five to twenty meteors per hour. Unlike other meteor showers, the source of the Sextantids is not a comet but an asteroid: asteroid 2005 UD, to be precise. Scientists believe that asteroid 2005 UD might be another break-off from a larger body. As the Earth passes through asteroid 2005 UD's trail, bits of debris burn up in our atmosphere and become shooting stars.

METEOR SHOWER

RECURS ANNUALLY

CAN BE SEEN WITH NAKED EYE

....

BEST VIEWING TIME: early morning before dawn

....

PEAK: 5–20 meteors per hour

....

DIRECTION IN SKY: east (though meteors can radiate across most of the sky)

....

DID YOU KNOW?
Each of Saturn's rings orbits the planet at a different speed.

77%

CONJUNCTION OF MOON AND SATURN

Saturn and the Moon will again be near each other in the night sky. Look towards the Moon, which should be in a southern direction above the horizon, and then look for a bright point nearby.

BEST VIEWING TIME: after dusk but before midnight

DIRECTION IN SKY: south

PLANETARY
EVENT

CAN BE
SEEN WITH
NAKED EYE

METEOR
SHOWER

RECURS
ANNUALLY

CAN BE
SEEN WITH
NAKED EYE

CAMELOPARDALIDS METEOR SHOWER

86%

The Camelopardalids occur when the Earth passes through the tail of comet 209P/LINEAR (once thought to be an asteroid). It's among the quietest showers of the year, with only around two meteors per hour even at its peak. The best time to view the shower is just before dawn near the North Star.

BEST VIEWING TIME: early morning before dawn

PEAK: 2 meteors per hour

DIRECTION IN SKY: north (though meteors can radiate across most of the sky)

DID YOU KNOW?
Jupiter is named for
the king of the Roman
gods, which makes
sense: it's *huge!*

98%

CONJUNCTION OF MOON AND JUPITER

A nearly full moon might make this conjunction a little harder to see. Look for a bright point near the Moon above the southern horizon around midnight.

BEST VIEWING TIME: **midnight**

DIRECTION IN SKY: **southeast**

PLANETARY
EVENT

CAN BE
SEEN WITH
NAKED EYE

RADIANT: Draco

100%

DRACONIDS METEOR SHOWER

METEOR SHOWER

RECURS ANNUALLY

CAN BE SEEN WITH NAKED EYE

Though typically a quieter meteor shower with around ten to twenty meteors per hour, the Draconids can sometimes be quite dramatic: observers in Europe counted over 600 meteors per hour in 2011! The source of the Draconids is the comet 21P/Giacobini-Zinner, which left a particularly condensed trail of dust and debris when it passed through the area in 1900.

BEST VIEWING TIME: just after dusk or right before dawn

PEAK: 10-20 meteors per hour

DIRECTION IN SKY: northwest (though meteors can radiate across most of the sky)

OCT
10

99%

SOUTHERN TAURIDS METEOR SHOWER

Though producing around only five meteors per hour, the Southern Taurids are a surprisingly steady meteor shower between September 10 and November 20 (yes, that long!) that produces a fair number of fireballs. Instead of looking for a peak in activity, which would technically be October 10, the best viewing time is actually when the Moon is new so that there is as little light interference as possible. This year, the Moon will be least visible on September 25 and October 25, so consider viewing on those dates instead.

BEST VIEWING TIME: just before dawn

PEAK: 5 meteors per hour

DIRECTION IN SKY: northeast (though meteors can radiate across most of the sky)

METEOR
SHOWER

RECURS
ANNUALLY

CAN BE
SEEN WITH
NAKED EYE

OCT 14

79%

PLANETARY EVENT

CAN BE SEEN WITH NAKED EYE

CONJUNCTION OF MOON AND MARS

Look for a bright point right near the Moon—that's Mars! You might notice its reddish color.

....

BEST VIEWING TIME: the two hours before dawn

....

DIRECTION IN SKY: south

....

OCT
21

ORIONIDS METEOR SHOWER

17%

Another meteor shower caused by Comet Halley (see the η-Aquariid meteor shower on May 6), the Orionids shower is a reliable fall favorite. The peak will happen around October 21 with roughly fifteen meteors per hour. The best viewing time is just before dawn. Thankfully, this year's shower peak will happen on a night where the Moon is just a sliver of a crescent, so light interference shouldn't be a problem. Meteors will radiate from around the Orion constellation (recognizable from the belt made of three stars close in a row).

METEOR
SHOWER

RECURS
ANNUALLY

CAN BE
SEEN WITH
NAKED EYE

BEST VIEWING TIME: just before dawn

PEAK: 15 meteors per hour

DIRECTION IN SKY: northeast (though meteors can radiate across most of the sky)

NOV
1

53%

CONJUNCTION OF MOON AND SATURN

PLANETARY
EVENT

CAN BE
SEEN WITH
NAKED EYE

If you have them, point your binoculars towards the Moon, which should be in a southern direction above the horizon. Look for a bright point nearby.

BEST VIEWING TIME: **after dusk but before midnight**

DIRECTION IN SKY: **south**

DID YOU KNOW? Jupiter's largest moons were discovered by Galileo in 1610. One is as large as Mercury, and another may have underground oceans!

CONJUNCTION OF MOON AND JUPITER

This is another chance to catch Jupiter passing nearby the Moon. Look for a bright point near the Moon above the southern horizon around midnight.

BEST VIEWING TIME: **midnight**

DIRECTION IN SKY: **south**

PLANETARY EVENT

CAN BE SEEN WITH NAKED EYE

NOV 8

☀ TOTAL LUNAR ECLIPSE

100%

LUNAR ECLIPSE

CAN BE SEEN WITH NAKED EYE

If you missed the total lunar eclipse on May 15, this is another chance to see one! Lunar eclipses happen with regularity, though a *total* lunar eclipse is more rare. This happens when the Earth moves between the Moon and the Sun, casting a shadow and causing the Moon to darken or turn red in color. This particular eclipse will be visible throughout America, Oceania, and Asia. It will begin around 1:00 am PST/4:00 am EST Sunday night. Gradually, as the Moon moves into Earth's shadow, the eclipse will grow until the Moon is in total darkness by 2:17 am PST/5:17 am EST. Unlike solar eclipses, a lunar eclipse can be viewed directly with the naked eye.

BEST VIEWING TIME: Between 1:00 am PST/4:00 am EST and 3:00 am PST/6:00 am EST

DID YOU KNOW? Over a dozen craft—from rovers to satellites—from different nations are currently on or orbiting around Mars. Apart from Earth, it's the most studied planet in our solar system.

NOV 11

CONJUNCTION OF MOON AND MARS

Look for a bright point near the Moon. If it has a reddish hue, that's likely Mars!

BEST VIEWING TIME: **the two hours before dawn**

DIRECTION IN SKY: **southwest**

PLANETARY EVENT

CAN BE SEEN WITH NAKED EYE

NOV 12

RADIANT: Taurus

85%

NORTHERN TAURIDS METEOR SHOWER

Cousin of the Southern Taurids (see October 10), the Northern Taurids are caused by the same comet (comet 2P/Encke). Scientists believe that Jupiter's gravitational pull may have warped the comet's trail into two streams. Hence, there is a Northern and Southern variety, with both showers overlapping and adding to the overall volume of meteors. The Taurids are known for producing particularly bright meteors, which some observers have dubbed "Halloween fireballs." As with the Southern Taurids, the Northern Taurids might be best viewed when there is no moon, which would be October 25 and November 23.

METEOR SHOWER

RECURS ANNUALLY

CAN BE SEEN WITH NAKED EYE

BEST VIEWING TIME: just before dawn

PEAK: 5 meteors per hour

DIRECTION IN SKY: northeast (though meteors can radiate across most of the sky)

RADIANT: Leo

NOV 17

 LEONIDS METEOR SHOWER 41%

The Leonids meteor shower promises to be especially spectacular this year. The shower will be active from November 6 through November 30, but the peak will occur on November 17 when some scientists predict as many as 250-300 meteors per hour! This is an unusual volume; the shower typically produces 15-20 at its peak. The comet Tempel-Tuttle is responsible for the shower, and it occasionally produces meteor storms with thousands of meteors every hour (though this isn't predicted for this year).

METEOR SHOWER

RECURS ANNUALLY

CAN BE SEEN WITH NAKED EYE

BEST VIEWING TIME: between midnight and dawn

PEAK: 250-300 meteors per hour!

DIRECTION IN SKY: east (though meteors can radiate across most of the sky)

NOV 21

8%

α-MONOCEROTIDS METEOR SHOWER

The Monocerotids meteor shower produces a modest volume of meteors, but it can vary widely year over year. Outbursts with hundreds or thousands of meteors every hour were observed in 1925, 1935, 1985, and 1995, and having one again depends on conditions being just right (it was predicted for 2019 but didn't come to pass). No such outburst is expected this year, but as with all meteor showers, the Monocerotids are unpredictable. It's little wonder that some stargazers call them "unicorn meteors," and not just because they radiate near Monoceros, the unicorn constellation!

METEOR SHOWER

RECURS ANNUALLY

CAN BE SEEN WITH NAKED EYE

BEST VIEWING TIME: between midnight and dawn

PEAK: varies

DIRECTION IN SKY: east (though meteors can radiate across most of the sky)

DID YOU KNOW? Saturn's rings were named alphabetically (Ring A, Ring B, and so on) in the order they were discovered, not the order in which they surround the planet.

CONJUNCTION OF MOON AND SATURN

27%

Saturn and the Moon will be close together in the night sky. Binoculars might make it easier to see. Point them towards the Moon, which should be in a southern direction above the horizon, and look for a bright point nearby.

BEST VIEWING TIME: **after dusk but before midnight**

DIRECTION IN SKY: **south**

PLANETARY EVENT

CAN BE SEEN WITH NAKED EYE

DEC
1

CONJUNCTION OF MOON AND JUPITER

60%

This is another chance to catch Jupiter passing nearby the Moon. Look for a bright point near the Moon above the southwest horizon between dusk and midnight.

BEST VIEWING TIME: **between dusk and midnight**

DIRECTION IN SKY: **southwest**

PLANETARY
EVENT

CAN BE
SEEN WITH
NAKED EYE

DID YOU KNOW? One day on Mars (called a *sol* instead of a day) lasts for 24.6 Earth hours.

CONJUNCTION OF MOON AND MARS

99%

One last chance to easily spot Mars this year! Mars and the Moon will be near each other in the night sky, making it simple to spot both at once. You can see them with the naked eye or with binoculars, but they might be too far apart to see through a telescope. As always, look for a bright point right near the Moon.

PLANETARY EVENT

CAN BE SEEN WITH NAKED EYE

BEST VIEWING TIME: **between dusk and dawn**

DIRECTION IN SKY: **north**

DEC 12

Hydra

84%

σ-HYDRIDS METEOR SHOWER

METEOR SHOWER

RECURS ANNUALLY

CAN BE SEEN WITH NAKED EYE

The Sigma Hydrids are slower in general, with around three meteors per hour at the shower's peak, but they're known for producing brighter-than-average meteors. They occur from December 3 through December 15, with the peak happening around December 12. For best viewing, watch the night sky between midnight and dawn in a northwestern direction (though, as with all meteor showers, meteors can radiate across most of the sky, so don't be too stressed about looking in the right direction).

BEST VIEWING TIME: between midnight and dawn

PEAK: 3 meteors per hour

DIRECTION IN SKY: northwestern (though meteors can radiate across most of the sky)

DEC 14

68%

⊛ GEMINIDS METEOR SHOWER

One of the best (and most reliable) meteor showers of the year, the Geminids take place between December 4 and December 17, with the peak occurring during the early morning of December 14 around 2 am. Forecasts predict as many as 120 meteors per hour during the peak, so this is one to watch. The Geminids occur when the Earth passes through the orbit of asteroid 3200 Phaethon (though some call it a "rock comet"), which was first discovered in 1983 when scientists were reviewing images taken by a satellite.

BEST VIEWING TIME: between midnight and dawn (2 am is best)

PEAK: 120 meteors per hour

DIRECTION IN SKY: east (though meteors can radiate across most of the sky)

METEOR SHOWER

RECURS ANNUALLY

CAN BE SEEN WITH NAKED EYE

DEC 16

METEOR SHOWER

RECURS ANNUALLY

CAN BE SEEN WITH NAKED EYE

COMAE BERENICIDS METEOR SHOWER

49%

Though it's one of the harder meteor showers to see—and one of the least active—it's worth mentioning the Comae Berenicids because they produce some of the fastest meteors in the night sky. Occurring between December 12 and December 23, the Comae Berenicids peak on December 16 with a zenith of around three meteors per hour.

BEST VIEWING TIME: between midnight and dawn

PEAK: 3 meteors per hour

DIRECTION IN SKY: southwest (though meteors can radiate across most of the sky)

RADIANT:

Leo Minor

DEC 20

DECEMBER LEONIS MINORIDS METEOR SHOWER

Not to be confused with the regular Leonis Minorids (see November 17), the December Leonis Minorids can produce up to five meteors per hour at its peak, which occurs on December 20. The shower itself lasts from December 5 until February 4. This year, there will be almost no Moon when the meteor shower peaks on December 20, so there's a better-than-average chance of seeing some of the shooting stars.

....

BEST VIEWING TIME: between midnight and dawn

....

PEAK: 5 meteors per hour

....

DIRECTION IN SKY: southwest (though meteors can radiate across most of the sky)

....

METEOR
SHOWER

RECURS
ANNUALLY

CAN BE
SEEN WITH
NAKED EYE

DECEMBER SOLSTICE

This marks the first day of winter in the Northern Hemisphere (hence it is sometimes called the winter solstice). It occurs when the northern pole of the Earth is pointed its furthest from the Sun. As a result, it is also the shortest day of the year, with cities in the extreme north experiencing darkness nearly all day—only four hours of light in Fairbanks, Alaska, and absolutely no light in Inuvik, Canada!—and cities further south having still less-than-usual light—just nine hours in Washington, DC, and only eight hours in London. But cheer up—from here on out, the days will keep getting longer until June.

ORBITAL
MILESTONE

RECURS
ANNUALLY

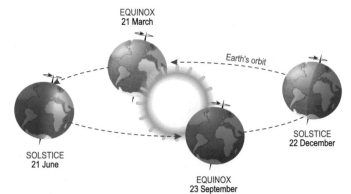

EQUINOX
21 March

Earth's orbit

SOLSTICE
22 December

SOLSTICE
21 June

EQUINOX
23 September

RADIANT: Ursa Minor

DEC 22

1%

URSIDS METEOR SHOWER

The Ursids are a chilly affair but, with its occasional bursts of activity, one that keeps people watching. Lasting from December 17 through December 26, the peak usually occurs near the December solstice. At its peak, the shower can produce ten meteors per hour, but rare bursts can sometimes reach up to one hundred. For best viewing, bundle up and head outdoors in the early hours just before dawn on December 22. The source of the Ursids is the trail of comet 8P/Tuttle (and if you think you've kept hearing "Tuttle," that's because you have: H. P. Tuttle and his brother were both active astronomers after the Civil War and responsible for many discoveries).

BEST VIEWING TIME: just before dawn

PEAK: 10 meteors per hour

DIRECTION IN SKY: north (though meteors can radiate across most of the sky)

METEOR SHOWER

RECURS ANNUALLY

CAN BE SEEN WITH NAKED EYE

CONJUNCTION OF MOON AND SATURN

14%

One last time, Saturn and the Moon will be near one another in the night sky. Look for a bright point near the Moon.

....

BEST VIEWING TIME: after dusk but before midnight

....

DIRECTION IN SKY: southwest

....

PLANETARY
EVENT

CAN BE
SEEN WITH
NAKED EYE

DEC 29

CONJUNCTION OF MOON AND JUPITER

44%

The final conjunction of the year! Look for a bright point near the Moon above the southwest horizon between dusk and midnight.

PLANETARY EVENT

CAN BE SEEN WITH NAKED EYE

BEST VIEWING TIME: **after dusk but before midnight**

DIRECTION IN SKY: **southwest**

ABOUT BUSHEL & PECK BOOKS

Bushel & Peck Books is a children's publishing house with a special mission. Through our Book-for-Book Promise™, we donate one book to kids in need for every book we sell. Our beautiful books are given to kids through schools, libraries, local neighborhoods, shelters, nonprofits, and also to many selfless organizations that are working hard to make a difference. So thank you for purchasing this book! Because of you, another book will make its way into the hands of a child who needs it most.

NOMINATE A SCHOOL OR ORGANIZATION TO RECEIVE FREE BOOKS

Do you know a school, library, or organization that could use some free books for their kids? We'd love to help! Please fill out the nomination form on our website (see below), and we'll do everything we can to make something happen.

www.bushelandpeckbooks.com/pages/
nominate-a-school-or-organization

If you liked this book, please leave a review online at your favorite retailer. Honest reviews spread the word about Bushel & Peck—and help us make better books, too!

Printed in the United States
by Baker & Taylor Publisher Services